Ghiberti's *Bronze Doors*

Ghiberti's
BRONZE DOORS

By Richard Krautheimer

PRINCETON, NEW JERSEY

PRINCETON UNIVERSITY PRESS

1971

Acknowledgment for photographs is made as follows:

Albertina, Vienna: 37
Alinari: 1-2, 51d
Brogi: 3-11, 14, 16-36, 38-48, 50, 51a-c, 51f-53c, 54b, 55b-58,
    60, 62-68, 69b, 70-91, 93-102, 104-106, 108-111, 113,
    115-117, 120-121, 123-125, 127-151a, 152-155
Clarence Kennedy: 15
Kunsthistorisches Institut, Universität Marburg: 51e, 69b
Rollie McKenna: 12-13, 49, 53d-f, 55a, 59, 61, 69a, c-d, 92,
    103, 107, 112, 114, 118-119

This book has been composed in Linotype Granjon

Printed in the United States of America
by Princeton University Press, Princeton, New Jersey

Illustrations by The Meriden Gravure Company
Meriden, Connecticut

Contents

Ghiberti's *Bronze Doors*

Isaac. Gates of Paradise (photo: Sansoni)

Ghiberti's *Bronze Doors*

T HE BAPTISTERY—Dante called it his lovely San Giovanni—has been the pride of Florence and admired by every visitor over these past nine hundred years. Built about 1050 and dedicated like all mediaeval baptisteries to Saint John the Baptist, it rises opposite the cathedral, at the northern edge of the mediaeval town: eight-sided, impressively simple, covered by a huge roofed dome, the doors facing east, north, and south. Its construction and maintenance rested with the guild of the big merchants, the *Calimala*. Powerful and wealthy, their committees financed and supervised the structure and vaulting; the splendid clothing of the walls, inside and out, in dark green and white marble; the glittering mosaics in the dome and over the chancel; the rich pavement; finally, in 1330, a bronze door cast by Andrea Pisano, showing in quatrefoils eight seated virtues and twenty scenes from the Life of John the Baptist. The door, an extraordinary feat at the time, was set up on the south gate, facing the approach from the center of the old town, from Piazza della Signoria.

Thus, work on San Giovanni had taken close to three hundred years. Slowed down, while attention was diverted to building and decorating the new cathedral and its tower, Giotto's *campanile*, the mind of all Florence by 1400 turned again to the Baptistery; the cathedral, excepting its dome, was near completion; but the Baptistery still lacked an integral part of its decoration. Its north and east gates, the latter facing the cathedral, still had to be provided with bronze doors, competing with Andrea's on the south. To tell fully the story of Salvation, one of these doors must represent scenes from the Gospels, the other from the Old Covenant. Thus, in 1401, the *Calimala* guild announced a competition for these doors. Seven artists were each invited to submit a trial piece in bronze within two years. Within a quatrefoil, like those on Andrea's door, it was to show the scene of *Abraham's Sacrifice* from the Book of Genesis. The artists invited were chosen with deliberation. They were sculptors and woodcarvers, goldsmiths and bell-founders; they came from Florence, from Siena, from Arezzo; most were old hands, aged thirty to fifty, excepting two just over twenty: Filippo Brunelleschi and Lorenzo Ghiberti. As it turned out, only the trial pieces of these two passed into the final screening and thus survived; they are now in the Bargello Museum. In the end, first prize—and with it the commission for one door and an option for the second—went to young Lorenzo: just twenty-two years old, with nothing but the trial piece to show for it; born out of wedlock, the son of the goldsmith Bartolo di Michele, whom his mother later married. 1,2

— Everybody in Florence and certainly the committee members must have known that they were taking an awful risk. The wealthiest guild, in charge of its most prominent building, was about to entrust to an untried youngster the costliest and most difficult piece of sculpture likely to be commissioned in Florence within a generation. Ghiberti in his autobiography

3

fifty years later still was flushed with pride by his victory over so many expert competitors. But at the time of the competition tensions went high among the Florentines, always a sensitive and excitable lot. Both Ghiberti's and Brunelleschi's trial pieces broke away from the somewhat stale late mediaeval formulas to which older Florentine artists and their public had become accustomed by 1400. Conservatives cried out and progressives were split between the partisans of Brunelleschi and Ghiberti. But the gentlemen of the *Calimala* guild knew what they liked in young Ghiberti's trial piece: they were impressed by his casting technique; they admired his precision in finishing; and they loved his way of telling a story.

The casting was done in what is called the "lost wax technique": the relief was modeled first in wax; the model then was packed in clay; liquid bronze was poured in; and, melting the wax, the bronze would fill the hollow form. Modeling and casting by this process went fast, and the emerging cast was thin-walled and in one piece. Also, it was durable and saved material and labor. The finishing of the rough cast, on the other hand, was time-consuming and it required full mastery of material and tools. Every form, figures and draperies, had to be smoothed and filed down to the tiniest details. Faces, hands and feet, eyes, ears, and curls were worked on with burins and fine chisels in months of painstaking labor, yet with constant alertness and inventiveness and with an absolutely sure hand. So in the contract the *Calimala* guild insisted on the young master's working "with his own hand . . . both in wax and in bronze"—that is in the modeling and the finishing stages—"figures, trees . . . hair, nudes and the like. . . ." Once chased to perfection, the relief was ready for fire gilding. The parts to be gilded were covered with gold dust, mixed with mercury; heated to 450 degrees Fahrenheit, the mercury evaporated while the gold particles clung to the bronze. The technical procedure throughout was grounded in the goldsmiths' craft, and Ghiberti had carried it through with a perfection uncanny in one so young. He was a goldsmith born and bred, and superbly trained in his craft.

At the same time, his relief showed that he was wide awake to what artists were up to both in Florence and far outside her confines. His workmanship as well as his figure style, both elegant and true to nature, recall nothing so much as French goldsmith work, the best at the time, and coveted alike by royalty and merchant princes, like the leaders of the *Calimala* guild. Its reflection in Ghiberti's trial piece would appeal to such internationally minded businessmen. Also, he had shown how well aware he was of the awakening interest in classical antiquity. The humanist-trained members of the committee must have been attracted by the reminders of ancient art, scattered through the trial piece: the head of Abraham, recalling Zeus; the body of Isaac, a Greek youth; the servants, inspired by a Roman sarcophagus. Finally, the story of the Sacrifice was told dramatically, yet clearly and with reticence: the loving glance of Abraham, his hesitating hand, the trusting look of the boy. The design was harmonious and in its beauty superior to anything done in Florence for nearly a century. To judge by his trial piece, Ghiberti's door would satisfy everybody: it would be solid and durable; it would please the most sophisticated taste; and it would overwhelm the man in the street through its sheer beauty, its narrative clarity, and the glitter of its gilding.

1,15

Sometime in 1404 Ghiberti assembled a crew of assistants—Donatello, just eighteen, was one; Ghiberti's father, Bartolo, about fifty years old, was another—and went to work. A New Testament door, as laid down in the contract, it now stands at the north gate of the Baptistery. Its pattern, as presumably specified, followed closely that of Andrea's door at the south 3, Diagram 1 gate. Twenty-eight square panels, four to each row, are held by a strong frame; into each panel is set a quatrefoil. The two bottom rows contain single, seated figures, the five upper rows many-figured scenes. The over-all theme is the story of Christ, as told in the Gospels and elucidated by the Fathers of the Church. Hence, Augustine, Jerome, Gregory, and 4-7 Ambrose occupy the bottom row. Above are the Evangelists, each marked by his symbol. 8-13 Finally, the life of Christ is told in twenty episodes: four from His childhood, starting with the panel of the *Annunciation to Mary* and ending with *Christ Among the Doctors*; six from 14, 16-21 His manhood, starting with the *Baptism* and the *Temptation* and leading to the *Raising of* 22-30 *Lazarus*; eight from the Passion, beginning with His *Entry into Jerusalem* and ending with 31-45 the *Crucifixion*; finally, His triumph over death, the *Resurrection* and the *Pentecost*. Placed at 46-47 the corners of the panels and on the frame itself, forty-eight heads look out from miniature 50-66 quatrefoils. They are meant to be prophets, but one is a self-portrait of Ghiberti: roughly 154 thirty-four years old, and looking undeniably a bit smug. Strips of foliage are soldered to the front frame, and frogs, lizards, grasshoppers and tiny snakes creep and hop among the leaves. 69, 70

Every figure and scene is filled with life, but movements and emotions are controlled. Gestures are sparse; the stories, as a rule, are told with but a few figures; action, more often than not, is conveyed by a glance rather than by movement. In the *Raising of Lazarus*, the corpse, to the left, rises stiffly from the cave; Christ, opposite, barely lifts a hand, looking down 30 at Martha; the Magdalene, at His feet, is all swooning submission; the onlookers hardly seem 29 to breathe. In the *Temptation*, Satan, his batwings spread, shrinks from Christ's quietly reject- 23, 48 ing gesture. In the *Way to Calvary*, both the soldiers and the women are very still, their 42, 44 emotions subdued; all is focused on Christ and the huge cross on His shoulders. Even the *Flagellation*, the most dramatic story, is told in a low key; brutality and ugliness, customary 36-38 in that scene, are carefully avoided.

The bodies throughout the reliefs, are nearly full-round. Nudes, heads, draperies and hair are finely chiseled. Settings are barely hinted at by a few props—a tree, a rock, a gate. Space 12, 25, 40 is suggested only by the interlocking of figures and by their movements. Gilded, props and figures stand against the dark bronze of the ground.

The technical difficulties involved in modeling, casting and chasing a huge door with its wealth of figures and minute details are hard to imagine. The quatrefoils, it appears, were modeled and cast one by one or in small batches, stretching over fifteen years. Designing the reliefs and modeling in wax the main figures remained, it seems, a task firmly in Ghiberti's hands. Finishing went on simultaneously; and there, as in the casting, the assistants came in. They certainly did the first smoothing of the rough cast; they probably worked figures and parts of lesser importance; while Ghiberti with his own hand, as he was required to do, chased the majority of the hundreds of tiny heads in the reliefs and the best among the prophets' heads. It took a good sense of organization to handle at the same time modeling, casting, chasing, and preparing new work. Moreover, the huge framework of the two wings of the door had to be cast, each composed of a skeleton frame, a back plaque, and a lattice frame in front decorated with foliage strips. Together, the wings are roughly fifteen feet high and eight feet wide, and weigh close to ten tons. The casting alone was quite a feat, not to mention the finishing. It required a large workshop; Ghiberti's, we know, contained sheds, a court-yard, presumably housing the furnaces, and offices. All told, work on the door took over twenty years. Only in 1424 was it set in place.

Needless to say, Ghiberti's art changed and matured over these twenty years. He had grown away from the figure style and composition of the Competition relief. Instead, he brought to Florence the precious, fragile figures hung with voluminous draperies, that by 1400 signaled a style that was spreading from France and Germany. This vogue—art historians call it the International Style—Ghiberti transposed into his own idiom, that combination of firmness and elegance, of reticence and immediacy. Around 1417, most of the reliefs and a goodly number of the prophets' heads had been cast and chased. Ghiberti was the busiest and probably the most popular artist in Florence. But just then he was challenged. Young sculptors, but a few years his junior—Donatello foremost—and their equally young patrons, Cosimo Medici among them, demanded an art more monumental and more outspoken; an art more Florentine, more fundamentally in search of the lost art of Classical Antiquity. They were not satisfied with the reminders of the Roman past scattered through Ghiberti's reliefs and among the heads on the frame: in the *Entry*, a woman servant from a sarcophagus; on the frame, the heads of barbarian warriors. Such mere quotations were to give way to a deeper understanding of the stance and functioning of a body; to the convincing presentation of depth and atmosphere in a relief; to greater forcefulness of gesture and mien—brutality, if need be. These, by implication, were the demands of the younger leaders.

There must have been much heated talk in Florence in these days. Some among the *avant-garde*, artists and patrons, certainly looked on Ghiberti's work as old-fashioned and as out of step with their own progressive demands. But his thinking was not really so far from that of the younger generation. All his working life he had striven to present convincingly human figures and their intelligible interaction. He could meet with conviction, on his own terms, the new demands: by the classical equilibrium of the *Flagellation*, centered on the nude figure of Christ; among the prophets' heads by the thoughtful expression he unex-pectedly gives to a head of *Caesar*. Alongside Donatello, alongside the architect Brunelleschi and the painter Masaccio, Ghiberti stood in the twenties in the forefront of the forming of the new style—the Early Renaissance. But where Donatello was dramatic and at times violent, Ghiberti remained persuasive through his very gentleness. The art of the Early Renaissance has many facets, and Ghiberti's reticent as well as Donatello's vehement language are both essential components in its formation.

When the New Testament door was set in place, Ghiberti was in his mid forties. What-ever some critics might have said, Florence as a whole was enthusiastic. They admired the

6

telling of the story, the elegance and firmness of the design, the workmanship and the technical perfection. No bronze foundry could compete with his and with the skillful team he had trained over the years. The *Calimala* guild had patiently put up with endless delays— Ghiberti never kept a deadline in his life—nor were they deterred by the expense, 22,000 gold florins, which was as much as the annual defense budget of the Florentine republic. It was a foregone conclusion that Ghiberti would be commissioned to design and cast the door still wanting at the Baptistery, and in 1425 he was. It was equally obvious that this door would present the story of the Old Testament. Only such a cycle would round out the over-all program, the Salvation of Mankind, envisaged for the three doors: Old Covenant and New Covenant, linked by the Life of the Baptist, who was after all both the last of the prophets and the forerunner of Christ. Also obviously, everybody expected the pattern of the new door to follow that of the two earlier ones, Andrea Pisano's and Ghiberti's own: eight figures in quatrefoils, prophets this time, in two rows at the bottom; and likewise in quatrefoils, twenty Old Testament scenes leading from Creation to the Judgment of Solomon, the latter reminiscent of the Last Judgment, the end of this world and the beginning of eternity.

As to the pattern though, general opinion was far off. When Lorenzo went to work in earnest, some years after signing the contract in 1425, he broke with established custom. Instead of condensing the biblical scenes into twenty small quatrefoils, he chose to tell the rich story of the Old Testament at leisure; in nearly forty scenes, arranged in ten large panels. *72, Diagram 2* The prophets, their number likewise increased and supplemented by more biblical heroes, were banished to the frame: twenty figures standing in niches and twenty-four heads jutting *131–51* out from roundels, among them portraits of Ghiberti and his son and helper Vittorio; finally, *152–53, 155* at the bottom and top of the frame, Adam and Eve and Noah and his wife, the first and *127–30* second parents of mankind. The panels, being so much larger than quatrefoils, were no longer given over to single scenes. Instead, they each recounted a full story from the Old Testament, told in a sequence of episodes: Genesis, presenting the Creation of Adam, that of Eve, the *73* Fall of Man and the Expulsion from the Garden; the story of Cain and Abel; Noah's Ark, *77, 83* his Sacrifice and his Shame; Abraham meeting the Angels and the Sacrifice of Isaac; the story *88* of Jacob and Esau told in seven episodes; Joseph's life; Moses receiving the Law and the *89, 95, 100* Daughters of Israel rejoicing; Joshua Crossing the Jordan into the Promised Land and the *108* conquest of Jericho; David slaying Goliath, the defeat of the Philistines and his Entry into *115* Jerusalem; lastly, in one single scene, the Meeting of the Queen of Sheba with Solomon. The *120* prominence given to the visit of the queen, come from afar to the wise king of Israel, explains itself presumably by the momentous political-religious event expected in Florence at just that time: the Union of the Eastern and Western Churches. Some learned advisor must have counseled Ghiberti.

To see familiar stories—and everyone at the time knew his Bible by heart—told with such wealth of detail, must have delighted the hearts of the Florentines. Ghiberti, when telling his own life, was rightly proud of this feat. He was even prouder of the way he had presented the tale persuasively to the eye: with that many episodes, as he says, all clearly visible; with that many figures, more than a hundred in some panels, leading from nearly full-round foreground figures to a very shallow relief. And all are shown in a seemingly deep and wide space, convincingly rendered in perspective, or, to use Ghiberti's words, "in the relation with which the eye measures them and [with] . . . the figures nearest larger and those farthest, smaller, as reality shows it." What Ghiberti meant to say was that on the panels of the new door he had set out to achieve in bronze what had, until then, been possible only in painting. The first to do so, he had broken through the boundaries of sculpture as previously understood. And he was filled with the pride of his achievement.

Indeed, his autobiography leaves us no doubt as to his ambition in designing the second door: to present a story, with many figures moving through deep landscapes and spacious architectural settings, bathed in atmosphere; and thus to convey, though on a small scale, the impression of both truthfulness and monumentality created by the great mural painters past and present. In the *Cain and Abel* panel the foreground figures—Cain ploughing with his yoke of oxen; Cain almost proudly bearing the curse of the Lord—are nearly full-round. In the second plane the relief has decreased: Abel seated on a knoll, watching his flock; Cain slaying his brother. Far in the rear, on a mountain top and in very shallow relief, yet clearly outlined, the brothers offer their sacrifice. To the left, in the same back plane, still babies, they play at the knees of their parents, seated before a straw hut. Trees and rocks link the planes; the shimmer of gold, all over figures, scenery and the empty ground, provides the illusion of an enveloping atmosphere. Similarly, in the *Noah* panel, the eye glides with ease from the strong scenes in the front plane, Noah's Sacrifice and his Shame, to the groups in the rear; the finely chased animals, lions and elephants and the birds fluttering about the top of the Ark, in a relief hardly raised from the ground. In the *Isaac* panel directly below, an architectural setting of classical design supplies the illusion of a deep and measurable space and provides a front stage and side stages for the various episodes: Isaac sending Esau on his wild goose chase; Jacob receiving his blessing, backed up by Rebecca; the women attending the birth of the twins; in the background, Rebecca in labor, the quarrel of the brothers; Rebecca's prayer; Esau hunting. The *Meeting of the Queen of Sheba* with Solomon finally, assembles all figures—close to a hundred—on the two levels of the stage: the royal couple in the middle, raised on a platform, their suites on either side; in the foreground, bystanders, on foot and horseback; all arranged like the chorus in a Greek tragedy or, for that matter, a Verdi opera.

Modeling and finishing panels with that many shades of relief and that many figures, not to speak of the designing or the work on the frame, required a dependable, well-trained and well-supervised workshop. Ghiberti's two sons, Tommaso and Vittorio, joined him; the number of assistants hired by the firm Lorenzo Ghiberti and sons grew. The old man himself still designed the layout of most of the panels. He also modeled in wax with his own hand the finest of the figures: Eve, rising towards the Lord; the four women in the story of *Jacob and Esau*; the distribution of the grain, to the right in the *Joseph* panel. But a goodly number of subordinate scenes was entrusted to assistants. Modeling and casting went quickly, it seems; within a few years from the start in 1436, all ten panels were ready for finishing. But the

8

chasing took time, and much of it was in the hands of the dozens of helpers around the workshop. Even so, including work on the frame, its figures and foliage decoration, the job of finishing and fire-gilding lasted another fifteen years, until 1452 when the door was set up in the place of honor, on the East gate opposite the cathedral.

The great public would know little of the difficulties, technical and other, Ghiberti had overcome. They would be astounded and pleased by the novelties of the design, easily understood: the clear telling of the stories; the large number of figures; their expressive actions; the convincing suggestion of space and atmosphere; the fine chasing of details; the rich gilding. Fellow artists and connoisseurs would realize fully the mastery of technical complexities and the boldness of Ghiberti's conquest of a new dimension in relief sculpture. They would be arrested by the novel ways in which the art of classical antiquity had now been absorbed and re-interpreted. To Ghiberti, working on the East door, the Roman sarcophagi and portrait busts he had known from his early youth told a new tale. They offered him no longer just models to be copied; rather, they were examples of nature purified, offering solutions to all kinds of problems difficult to cope with: action, movement, the nude. They reflected a higher world, peopled by a different race of human beings: clad in flowing garments, slender, stepping lightly with graceful gestures. These concepts had become so natural to Ghiberti that he invented freely in the spirit of antiquity: Cain standing before the Lord like a Greek shepherd; Joseph revealing himself to his brethren; Isaac giving to Jacob the blessing fraudulently obtained; Eve being expelled from Paradise.

Ghiberti, at seventy, could look back with satisfaction. His had been a good life. He had prospered; bronze casters in Florence were well paid—as highly as bank managers. He was a wealthy man, owner of a little château, bought from an old patrician family, and other landed property. He was a respected citizen, notwithstanding the handicap of being born out of wedlock. As an artist he had made his mark and left a life's work of enduring beauty. In his workshop he had trained nearly all the sculptors of the younger generation. He was one of the founding fathers of the new style that by 1450 was spreading all over Italy. He was proud of what he had done. But he had tasted reverses as well and learned to bear them; the smugness of earlier years was gone. Thus in his late self-portrait he looks to be a wise, old man, shrewd and with a twinkle in his eye.

The gilding of the doors was to fifteenth century Florentines, as it is today, a decisive and perhaps to many the most decisive feature of the doors. One easily forgets that only twenty-five years ago hardly anyone suspected that wealth of shimmering gold. It was resurrected in its pristine beauty only after the Second World War, when Bruno Bearzi and his crew removed a layer of grime and oxidized bronze from the gilded surface. The gilding as much as their beauty may have caused the East doors, across from the cathedral, to be named the *Gates of Paradise*. Michelangelo supposedly coined the phrase. As the Italians say—*Se non è vero, è ben trovato*: true or not, it's a good story.

9

Way to Calvary, 42 Christ, 43 Mary and St. John, 44	*Crucifixion,* 45	*Resurrection,* 46	*Pentecost,* 47
Agony in the Garden, 33	*Arrest,* 34	*Flagellation,* 38 Christ at the Column, 36	*Pilate,* 39 Pilate and Servant, 41
Transfiguration, 27 Apostles, 28	*Raising of Lazarus,* 30 Mary Magdalene, 29 Man at Left, 35	*Entry,* 31	*Last Supper,* 32
Baptism, 22 Angels, 40	*Temptation,* 23 Wing of Satan, 48	*Expulsion,* 24 Fallen Youth, 25	*Christ in the Storm,* 26
Annunciation, 14 Mary, 16	*Nativity,* 17	*Adoration of the Magi,* 18 Holy Family, 19	*Christ among the Doctors,* 20 Right Side of Panel, 21
Saint John, 8 Eagle, 12	*Saint Matthew,* 9 Detail, 13 Wing of Angel, 49	*Saint Luke,* 10	*Saint Mark,* 11
Saint Augustine, 4	*Saint Jerome,* 5	*Saint Gregory,* 6	*Saint Ambrose,* 7

DIAGRAM 1. Schema of the North Door (Pl. 3)

Eve, 127	Adam, 129

Genesis, 73 Adam, 74 Eve, 75 Expulsion, 76 Lord with Angelic Host, 104	**Cain and Abel, 77** Slaying of Abel, 78 Cursing of Cain, 79 Cain Plowing, 80 First Parents, 81
Noah, 83 Animals Leaving the Ark, 82 Noah's Drunkenness, 84 Noah's Sacrifice, 87 Noah's Sons, 86 Noah Leaving the Ark, 102	**Abraham, 88** Servants Waiting, 85 Trees, 106
Isaac, 89 Rebecca Praying, 90 Esau and His Dogs, 91 Visiting Women, 93 Blessing of Jacob, Rebecca, 94	**Joseph, 95** Distribution of Grain, 96 Architectural Detail, 97 Joseph Revealing Himself, 98 Two Girls, 99 Corn Hall, 124
Moses, 100 Daughters of Israel, 101 People at Mt. Sinai, 103 Moses Receiving the Law, 105 Trees, 107	**Joshua, 108** Carrying of the Stones, 109-10 Joshua on Chariot, 111 Group, 112 Walls of Jericho, 113
David, 115 Right Side of Panel, 116 Detail, 117 Entry into Jerusalem, 118 Palm Tree, 119 Jerusalem, 114	**Solomon, 120** Falconer with Dog, 92 Solomon and Queen of Sheba, 121 Group upper right, 122 Group lower right, 123 Architectural Detail, 125
Noah, 128	Puarphera, 130

DIAGRAM 2. Schema of the Gates of Paradise (Pl. 72)

List of Illustrations

COLOR PLATES

PLATES

101. *Moses*, Daughters of Israel. Gates of Paradise
102. *Noah*, Noah and His Family Leaving the Ark. Gates of Paradise
103. *Moses*, The People at Mount Sinai. Gates of Paradise
104. *Genesis*, The Lord with the Angelic Host. Gates of Paradise
105. *Moses*, Moses Receives the Law. Gates of Paradise
106. *Abraham*, Trees. Gates of Paradise
107. *Moses*, Trees. Gates of Paradise
108. *Joshua*. Gates of Paradise
109. *Joshua*, The Carrying of the Stones. Gates of Paradise
110. *Joshua*, The Carrying of the Stones. Gates of Paradise
111. *Joshua*, Joshua on Chariot. Gates of Paradise
112. *Joshua*, Group. Gates of Paradise
113. *Joshua*, The Walls of Jericho. Gates of Paradise
114. *David*, Jerusalem. Gates of Paradise
115. *David*. Gates of Paradise
116. *David*, right side. Gates of Paradise
117. *David*, Detail. Gates of Paradise
118. *David*, Entry into Jerusalem. Gates of Paradise
119. *David*, Palm Tree. Gates of Paradise
120. *Solomon*. Gates of Paradise
121. *Solomon*, Solomon and the Queen of Sheba. Gates of Paradise
122. *Solomon*, Group upper right. Gates of Paradise
123. *Solomon*, Group lower right. Gates of Paradise
124. *Joseph*, Corn Hall. Gates of Paradise
125. *Solomon*, Architectural Detail. Gates of Paradise
126. *Aaron*, Detail. Gates of Paradise
127. *Eve*. Gates of Paradise
128. *Noah*. Gates of Paradise
129. *Adam*. Gates of Paradise
130. *Puarphera*. Gates of Paradise
131. *Ezechiel* (?). Gates of Paradise
132. *Jeremiah* (?). Gates of Paradise
133. *Prophetess*. Gates of Paradise
134. *Joab* (?). Gates of Paradise
135. *Elia* (?). Gates of Paradise
136. *Jonah*. Gates of Paradise
137. *Hannah* (?). Gates of Paradise
138. *Samson*. Gates of Paradise
139. *Prophetess and Prophets*. Gates of Paradise
140. *Miriam*. Gates of Paradise

Competition Relief, detail, enlarged. Florence, Bargello (photo: Scala)

1. Ghiberti, Competition Relief. Florence, Bargello

2. Brunelleschi, Competition Relief. Florence, Bargello

3. North Door. Florence, Baptistery

5. *Saint Jerome.* North Door

4. *Saint Augustine.* North Door

7. *Saint Ambrose. North Door*

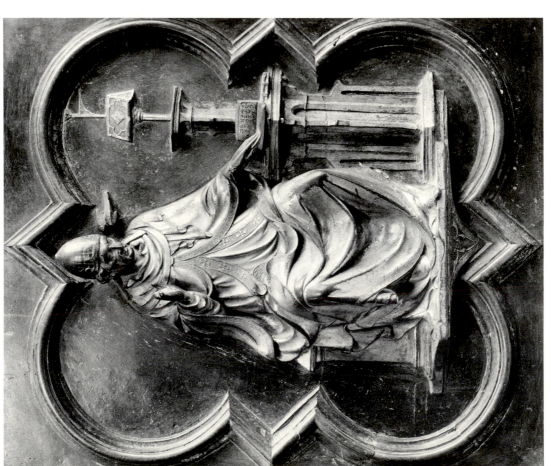

6. *Saint Gregory. North Door*

9. *Saint Matthew.* North Door

8. *Saint John the Evangelist.* North Door

11. *Saint Mark.* North Door

10. *Saint Luke.* North Door

12. *Saint John the Evangelist*, Eagle. North Door

13. *Saint Matthew*, Detail. North Door

14. *Annunciation*. North Door

15. Competition Relief, Isaac.
Florence, Bargello

16. *Annunciation*, Mary. North Door

17. *Nativity*. North Door

18. *Adoration of the Magi.* North Door

19. *Adoration of the Magi*, Holy Family. North Door

20. *Christ Among the Doctors.* North Door

21. *Christ Among the Doctors*, right half. North Door

22. *Baptism of Christ.* North Door

23. *Temptation*. North Door

24. *Expulsion of the Money Changers.* North Door

25. *Expulsion of the Money Changers*, Fallen Youth. North Door

26. *Christ in the Storm*. North Door

27. *Transfiguration.* North Door

29. *Raising of Lazarus*, Mary Magdalene. North Door

30. *Raising of Lazarus*. North Door

31. *Entry into Jerusalem.* North Door

32. *Last Supper*. North Door

33. *Agony in the Garden.* North Door

34. *Arrest of Christ.* North Door

35. *Raising of Lazarus*, Man at Left.
North Door

36. *Flagellation*, Christ at the Column.
North Door

37. *Flagellation*, Sketch. Vienna, Albertina

38. *Flagellation.* North Door

39. *Christ before Pilate.* North Door

41. *Christ before Pilate, Pilate. North Door*

40. *Baptism of Christ, Angels. North Door*

42. *Way to Calvary.* North Door

43. *Way to Calvary*, Christ.
North Door

44. *Way to Calvary*, Mary and Saint John.
North Door

45. *Crucifixion*, North Door

46. *Resurrection.* North Door

47. *Pentecost.* North Door

48. *Temptation*, Wing of Satan. North Door

49. *Saint Matthew*, Wing of Angel. North Door

c

f

b

e

51. *Prophets*. North Door

a

d

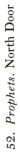

52. *Prophets. North Door*

a

b

c

d

e

f

53. *Prophets*. North Door

a

b

c

d

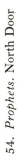

e

f

54. *Prophets*. North Door

c

b

a

f

e

d

55. *Prophets.* North Door

57. *Youthful Prophet.* North Door

56. *Elderly Prophetess.* North Door

Prophet, enlarged. North Door (photo: Fabbri)

59. *Youthful Prophet. North Door*

58. *Prophet. North Door*

61. *Prophet.* North Door

60. *Prophet.* North Door

63. *Youthful Prophetess. North Door*

62. *Youthful Prophet. North Door*

65. *Prophet. North Door*

64. *Youthful Prophetess. North Door*

66. *Prophet.* North Door

68. *Tondo*, back frame. Gates of Paradise

67. *Lion's Head*, back frame. North Door

d

c

69. Floral Decorations. North Door

b

a

70. Architrave Detail. North Door

71. Architrave Detail, outer jambs. Gates of Paradise

72. Gates of Paradise. Florence, Baptistery

73. *Genesis*. Gates of Paradise

74. *Genesis*, Adam. Gates of Paradise

75. *Genesis*, Creation of Eve. Gates of Paradise

76. *Genesis*, Expulsion from Paradise. Gates of Paradise

77. *Cain and Abel.* Gates of Paradise

79. *Cain and Abel*, Cursing of Cain. Gates of Paradise

78. *Cain and Abel*, Slaying of Abel. Gates of Paradise

80. *Cain and Abel*, Cain Plowing. Gates of Paradise

81. *Cain and Abel*, First Parents of Mankind. Gates of Paradise

82. *Noah*, Animals Leaving the Ark. Gates of Paradise

83. *Noah*. Gates of Paradise

84. *Noah*, Noah's Drunkenness. Gates of Paradise

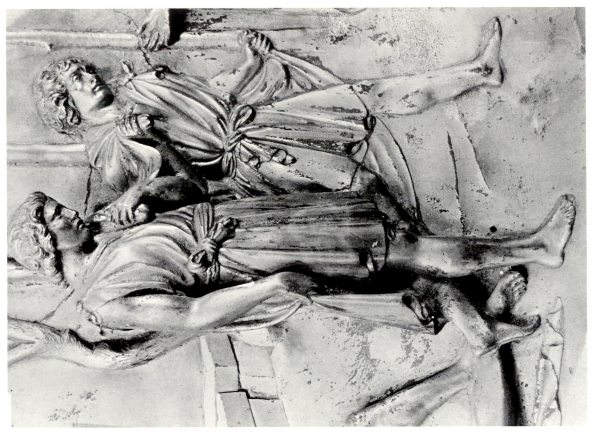

86. *Noah, Noah's Sons. Gates of Paradise*

85. *Abraham, Servants Waiting. Gates of Paradise*

87. *Noah*, Noah's Sacrifice, Detail. Gates of Paradise

88. *Abraham*. Gates of Paradise

LAVRENTII CIONIS DE GHIBERTIS

89. *Isaac*. Gates of Paradise

90. *Isaac*, Rebecca Praying. Gates of Paradise

92. *Solomon*, Falconier with Dog. Gates of Paradise

91. *Isaac*, Esau and His Dogs. Gates of Paradise

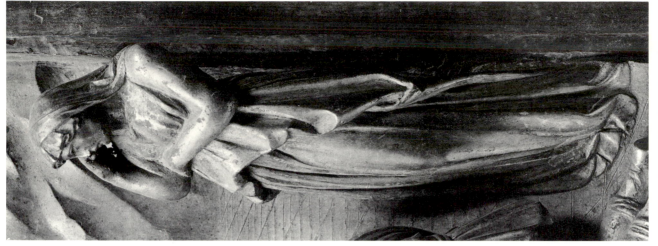

94. *Isaac*, Blessing of Jacob, Rebecca. Gates of Paradise

93. *Isaac*, Visiting Women. Gates of Paradise

95. *Joseph*. Gates of Paradise

96. *Joseph*, Distribution of Grain. Gates of Paradise

97. *Joseph*, Architectural Detail. Gates of Paradise

99. *Joseph*, Two Girls. Gates of Paradise

98. *Joseph*, Joseph Revealing Himself. Gates of Paradise

100. *Moses*. Gates of Paradise

101 *Moses*, Daughters of Israel. Gates of Paradise

102. *Noah*, Noah and His Family Leaving the Ark. Gates of Paradise

103. *Moses*, The People at Mount Sinai. Gates of Paradise

104. *Genesis*, The Lord with the Angelic Host. Gates of Paradise

105. *Moses*, Moses Receives the Law. Gates of Paradise

107. *Moses*, Trees. Gates of Paradise

106. *Abraham*, Trees. Gates of Paradise

108. *Joshua*. Gates of Paradise

110. *Joshua*, The Carrying of the Stones. Gates of Paradise

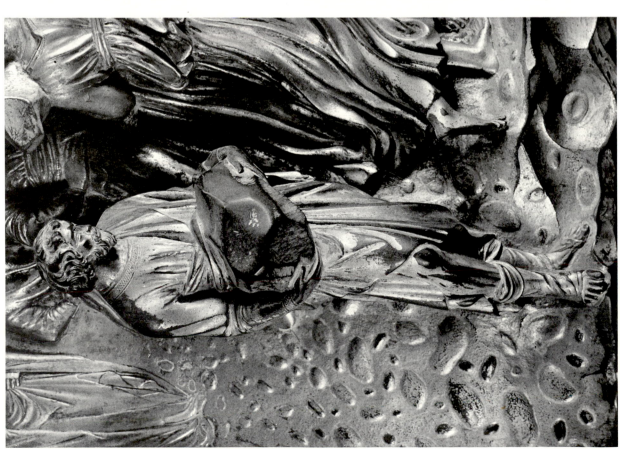

109. *Joshua*, The Carrying of the Stones. Gates of Paradise

111. *Joshua*, Joshua on Chariot. Gates of Paradise

112. *Joshua*, Group. Gates of Paradise

113. *Joshua*, The Walls of Jericho. Gates of Paradise

114. *David*, Jerusalem. Gates of Paradise

115. *David*. Gates of Paradise

116. *David*, right side. Gates of Paradise

117. *David*, Detail. Gates of Paradise

118. *David*, Entry into Jerusalem. Gates of Paradise

119. *David*, Palm Tree. Gates of Paradise

120. *Solomon*. Gates of Paradise

121. *Solomon*, Solomon and the Queen of Sheba. Gates of Paradise

122. *Solomon*, Group upper right. Gates of Paradise

123. *Solomon*, Group lower right. Gates of Paradise

124. *Joseph*, Corn Hall. Gates of Paradise

125. *Solomon*, Architectural Detail. Gates of Paradise

126. *Aaron*, Detail. Gates of Paradise

127. *Eve*. Gates of Paradise

128. *Noah*. Gates of Paradise

129. *Adam*. Gates of Paradise

130. *Puarphera*. Gates of Paradise

131. *Ezechiel* (?). Gates of Paradise   132. *Jeremiah* (?). Gates of Paradise

133. *Prophetess*. Gates of Paradise

134. *Joab* (?). Gates of Paradise

135. *Elia* (?). Gates of Paradise   136. *Jonah*. Gates of Paradise

137. *Hannah* (?). Gates of Paradise

138. *Samson*. Gates of Paradise

139. *Prophetess and Prophets. Gates of Paradise*

143. *Gideon* (?). Gates of Paradise

142. *Joshua*. Gates of Paradise

141. *Aaron*. Gates of Paradise

140. *Miriam*. Gates of Paradise

147. *Bileam* (?). Gates of Paradise

146. *Daniel* (?). Gates of Paradise

145. *Nathan* (?). Gates of Paradise

144. *Judith*. Gates of Paradise

148. *Prophets' Heads. Gates of Paradise*

149. *Prophets' Heads*. Gates of Paradise

150. *Prophets' Heads*. Gates of Paradise

c

f

b

e 151. *Prophets' Heads.* Gates of Paradise

a

d

153. Portrait of *Vittorio Ghiberti*. Gates of Paradise

152. *Lorenzo Ghiberti*, Self Portrait, Profile. Gates of Paradise

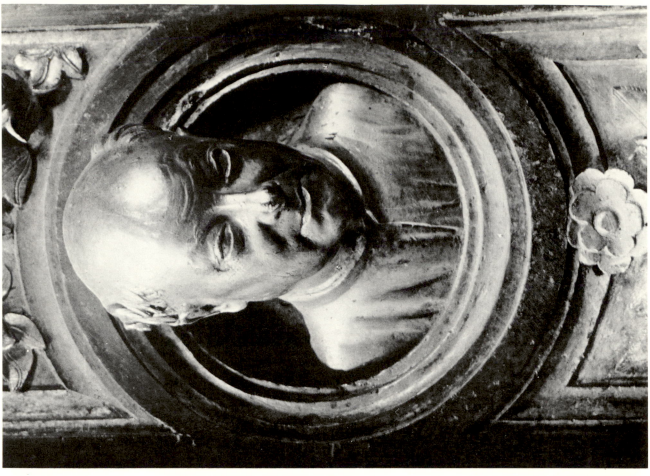

155. *Lorenzo Ghiberti*, Self Portrait. Gates of Paradise

154. *Lorenzo Ghiberti*, Self Portrait. North Door

Lorenzo Ghiberti, self-portrait, enlarged. Gates of Paradise (photo: Scala)